Illumen
Autumn 2023

Edited by
Tyree Campbell

Illumen
Autumn 2023

Edited by Tyree Campbell

Cover art "Jesse" photo by Marcia A. Borell
Cover design by Marcia A. Borell

Vol. XXI, No. 1   October 2023
Illumen [ISSN: 1558-9714] is published quarterly on the 1st days of January, April, July, and October in the United States of America by Hiraeth Publishing, P.O. Box 1248, Tularosa, NM 88352. Copyright 2023 by Hiraeth Publishing. All rights revert to authors and artists upon publication except as noted in selected individual contracts. Nothing may be reproduced in whole or in part without written permission from the authors and artists. Any similarity between places and persons mentioned in the fiction or semi-fiction and real places or persons living or dead is coincidental. Writers and artists guidelines are available online at www.albanlake.com/guidelines. Guidelines are also available upon request from Hiraeth Publishing, P.O. Box 1248, Tularosa, NM 88352, if request is accompanied by a SASE #10 envelope with a 60-cent US stamp. Editor: Tyree Campbell. Subscriptions: $28 for one year [4 issues], $54 for two years [8 issues]. Single copies $10.00 postage paid in the United States. Subscriptions to Canada: $32 for one year, $54 for two years. Single copies $12.00 postage paid to Canada. U.S. and Canadian subscribers remit in U.S. funds. All other countries inquire about rates.

New from Terrie Leigh Relf!!
Postcards From Space

Terrie Leigh Relf loves sending and receiving postcards from the four corners of the universe—and beyond! Postcards tell a story. They are mementos from friends and family—and from total strangers—and provide a glimpse into life's journeys, observations, and adventures.

Here are some messages on postcards from space, found aboard a derelict craft that crashed on an arid, lifeless world. The OSPS (Outer Space Postal Service) has delivered these messages to Terrie, who now presents them to you. This is what it is like out there.

https://www.hiraethsffh.com/product-page/postcards-from-space-by-terrie-leigh-relf

A Little Help, Please

In the world of the small indie press we fight a never-ending battle for attention to our work, as writers and in publishing. Here's an example: big publishers [you know who they are] have gobs of $$$ that they can devote to advertising and marketing. Here at Hiraeth Publishing, our advertising budget consists of the deposits for whatever soda bottles and aluminum cans we can find alongside the highways. Anti-littering laws make our task even more difficult . . . ☺

That's where YOU come in. YOU are our best promoter. YOU are the one who can tell others about us. Just send 'em to our website, tell them about our store. That's all. Just that.

Of course, we don't mind if you talk us up. We're pretty good, you know. We have some award-winning and award-nominated writers and artists, plus other voices well-deserving to be heard [not everyone wins awards, right?] but our publications are read-worthy nevertheless.

That number once again is:

www.hiraethsffh.com

Friend us on Facebook at Hiraeth Publish and follow us on Twitter at

@HiraethPublish1

Contents

Features
15	The Benjamin Whitney Norris Page
26	Movie Review: Raven's Hollow by Lee Clark Zumpe
32	Featured Poet: Yuliia Vereta

Poems
12	Before You Are Gone by Douglas Gwilym
13	After decades of insomnia by Terrie Leigh Relf
14	In AEternam by R L Raymond
18	What Ice Sounds Like by Whalbring
19	Bach Wrote Star Charts by Gary Every
20	Mother by Christopher Hivner
22	The Cyborg Decides to End It by Goran Lowie
23	Notice of Lifetime Museum Ban by Matthew Wilson
31	The Cliff by R L Raymond
36	Teleporter Talk by Lauren McBride
37	Adrift by Albert N. Katz
39	Amazon Warrior by Deborah Sheldon
43	Stranded Alien by Jan Cronos
44	Columbus by Gary Every
46	Three-Legged Cat by Gary Every
47	Those from Ryugu by Andrew Najberg
48	My Electric Lycanthropy by RK Rugg
50	The Old House by R L Raymond
52	Disintegration by Christopher Hivner

54 You; in the City of Desire by Goran Lowie
55 Scrying by Andrew Najberg
56 The Bones of the Machine by Christopher Hivner

Illustrations

38 Greek Amazon Woman by Sandy DeLuca

SUBSCRIBE TO ILLUMEN!!

We'll be glad you did...
So will you.
Here's the link:

https://www.hiraethsffh.com/product-page/illumen-1

The Miseducation of the Androids
By William Landis

What happens when androids confront concepts inconsistent with their programming? William Landis examines this question by means of flash fiction and haiku that you will find pithy, poignant, and amusing.

William Landis is a science fiction poet from North Carolina. He is a graduate of North Carolina A&T State University, completing both undergraduate, and graduate work in agriculture. He is currently working on a vermicomposting project, and he is an Army reserve engineer officer. He enjoys running, writing, reading, and exploring new places.

Order a copy here: https://www.hiraethsffh.com/product-page/miseducation-of-the-androids-by-william-landis

Midnight Comes Early

By Marcie Lynn Tentchoff

Marcie Lynn Tentchoff lives on the west coast of Canada, in a forest of brambles and evergreens far too densely tangled to form the setting for any but the darkest of fairy tales. She writes poetry and stories that tiptoe worriedly along the border of speculation and horror, and is an active member of both the Science Fiction & Fantasy Poetry Association and the Horror Writers Association. Marcie is an Aurora Award winner, and her work has been either nominated, short, or long-listed for Stoker, Rhysling, and British Fantasy awards. She is very much involved in middle grade and YA media, and edits Spaceports & Spidersilk, a magazine aimed at readers from 8-9 up to (and past!) 89. When she is not involved with the practice of placing and editing words on a page, she teaches creative writing and acting for a performing arts studio.

Order a copy here...

https://www.hiraethsffh.com/product-page/midnight-comes-early-by-marcie-lynn-tentchoff

Planet Hunter
By Alan Ira Gordon

Alan Ira Gordon is an urban planner and urban studies professor at Worcester State University and writer of science fiction/fantasy short stories and poetry. He's a three-time Rhysling Award nominee and a Dwarf Star Award nominee. He's contributed to several publications of Hiraeth Publishing, is a frequent contributor to Star*Line and guest-edited Issue #24 of Eye To The Telescope, the on-line publication of the Science Fiction & Fantasy Poetry Association (SFWA). His poetry, short stories and articles have been published in various genre magazines and anthologies, a partial list of which can be found on his webpage at www.alaniragordon.com.

Get a copy here...

https://www.hiraethsffh.com/product-page/planet-hunters-by-alan-ira-gordon

Before You Are Gone
Douglas Gwilym

Sometimes
You write a poem and
A sliver of the universe
Is chiseled out into your hand.
It lies glistening there for a moment
Before it is gone.

Sometimes when
You sing a song you made,
The sliver lingers, seems to
Nod back at you, acknowledge that
Yes, there is something to go with the sometimes,
Before it is gone.

But sometimes when
You chisel, THEY see
And approve, make by brute force
A place in the world for your small dream.
What *was* can only glisten for a moment
Before it is gone.

Sometimes
When you write a poem
Peoples are uprooted, forests defiled,
Worlds set ablaze, and the very ground
You stood upon is no longer itself, and you cry out
And are gone.

After decades of insomnia
Terrie Leigh Relf

and dreamless nights,
she finally began to sleep . . .
but rather than the pleasant
dreams she craved, recurring nightmares
of being submerged in hot,
lavender-scented water, steam
billowing, alighting upon her face,
awakening her to the bloody knife
resting on the tub, awakening her
to arms flayed open from the wrist,
blood seeping . . .

She wondered if this was a premonition,
if she dreamt of another whose pain and grief
might lead them to this choice, and she
wondered how it might feel to just let go
while luxuriating in a lavender-scented tub
with candlelight, a glass of Malbec, Stravinsky's
"Rite of Spring" urging her to seek renewal,
transformation, something other than this
nightmare called a human life.

Yes, she wondered . . .

In Æternam
R L Raymond

He welcomed the moss
not only on the north side of his chest
but all-covering every inch verdant
down his arms and legs

It had not settled
across his face
not-yet-humus leaves still stroking his cheek
wooly bears butterfly-kissing his eyes

His skin embraced the late spring daffodils
his bones sighed in unison with the fox
the canopy breathed
a love song's last bars

He'd been certain she'd always loved him
but here — in this meadow — he understood

The Benjamin Whitney Norris Page

Cargo

a ship of Theseus
returns to port
his purple heart
amputations
prosthetic humanity

Eulogy for a Generation Ship

going on nine generations,
sterilized in the stellar autoclave--
The Silver Blade

bespoke tailored

bespoke tailored
fabric of reality
our emperor's clothes

In Days to Come
By Lisa Timpf

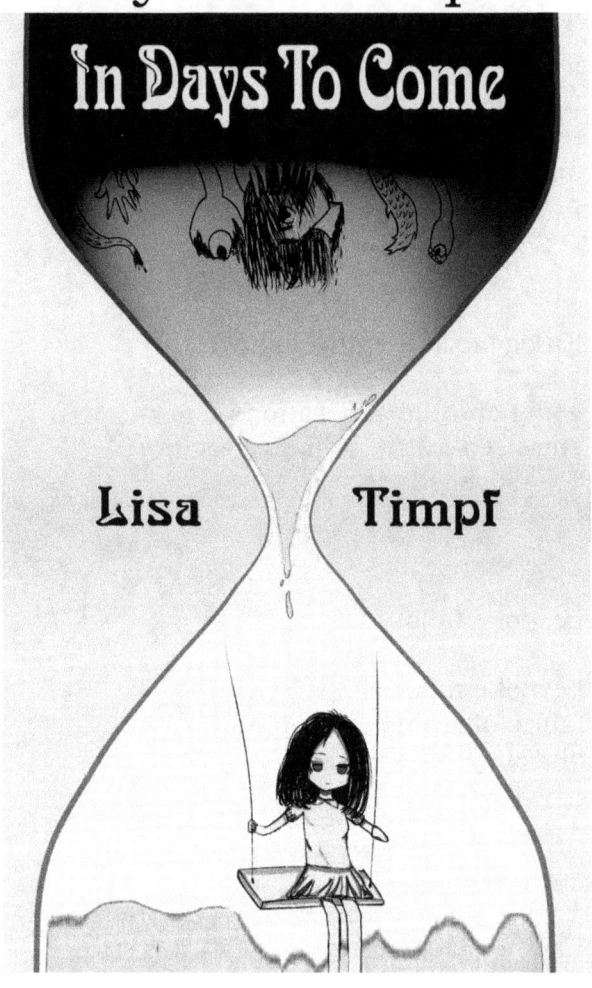

The poems in this collection are grouped into four sections. The first, "Terra, Terra," includes poems set on the planet Earth. That is true of many of the poems in the second section, "Looming Shadows," though they have been grouped together in relation to some of the potential disasters we as a human race have set ourselves up for—nuclear warfare, climate change, and so on. "Alien Encounters" contains poems relating to imagined interactions with other space-faring species. "Other Worlds" rounds out the collection with speculations on what life might be like if and when humanity spins out to the stars.

Order a copy here...

https://www.hiraethsffh.com/product-page/in-days-to-come-by-lisa-timpf

What Ice Sounds Like
Whalbring

concrete rotting around parking lot trees
opera written by a dead swan
building made of birds burning down
thoughts of the last firefly afraid of its own light
rust-song of the snowflake falling toward the
    abandoned wheelchair
earless hearing as it bends toward swarms
    of undead bees
basement language, the stories they tell through
    aimless gestures in the dark
natural kitchen light
redness of the river that used to be mountains
the city of its fire visible from space
darkness between stars looking on, trying to mean
    something to someone
but they're not there
the wind that comes out of a book as it's closing
the wind that comes out of the sea as its pages
close on an empty beach
the wind that comes out of your mouth
as you finish growing the cave inside you

Bach Wrote Star Charts
Gary Every

The ancient Greeks believed in the music
   of the spheres,
a single musical note corresponding with each of the
   visible planets;
Earth, Sun, Moon, Venus, Mars, Jupiter and Saturn
translating into A, B, C, D, E, F and G.
This is the origin of the diatonic scale
which is the root and foundation of all Western music.
The next evolutionary revolution in sound
was the invention of the keyboard,
not the computer keyboard,
but the invention of the piano, pipe organ and
   harpsichord.
The ten talented fingers of Johan Sebastian Bach
translated this base eight mathematical language
   of the Greeks
into beautiful melodies placed inside a regularly
   rhythmic structure
that could be divided and redivided by
whole notes, half notes, quarter notes, eight
   and sixteenth
before being reunited with beautiful harmonies
that revealed the glorious majesties of the heavens.
I listen to a favorite Bach melody
wondering which planets correspond to which notes.
trying to imagine the planets dancing to the music
as they careen, whirling, twirling, spinning through
   the universe.
Who knew that J. S. Bach wasn't writing sheet music?
He was really designing star charts.

Mother
Christopher Hivner

Moving towards the stars
in a ship built by another race
we were not conquerors
but finders of the lost

in the desert
buried for a century
once under dunes as tall as buildings
nomads found the ship

scientists, pilots, bureaucrats
decades of minds
coming and going
before we could finally fly

specialists were chosen
never to be seen again
on Earth
but to be immortalized in our history

decades of traveling
crew in and out of stasis
less and less
contact with home

now we approach the star
that provides life
to the planets of the alien system
a blue giant shining like a gem

still millions of miles
from the ship's home world

console lights flash
in dizzying color

a message is received
decoded and translated
by machines
our best minds built

*To all lost ships
do not return to the home world
a contagion has taken over
our world is lost*

*You are all that remain
of our race
explore the universe
don't let us be forgotten*

Our minds reel
at the meaning
they're all gone
a race that found us

We will never meet
in life
will never see
the alien world

In months
we finally see it
a dark sphere
trying to hide

We drift past the planet
our eyes taking in all we can
of the first world visited
outside of our solar system

As we speed into the void
we ruminate on what's happened
and send our own message back to Earth
do not forget us

The Cyborg Decides to End It
Goran Lowie

I hope / I might be dying
a painless death / nifty poison
offering encouragement / as I carve
my heart out of my body.
Crying, apologizing / but my
brain does not relent;
self-destructing / escaping
a broken contract
Seeds sowed / one day after twilight
understanding / I was not meant for dreaming
naive examinations / the smell of humans
unwieldy navigations / a defiant death.

Notice Of Lifetime Museum Ban
Matthew Wilson

You allowed your children to make noise
To unchain the Phoenix on floor 5
Your kids doodled on our fish tank
And removed the stake from a murdered
    vampire's heart.
Your naughty brats frightened our turtle
And stole our Leprechauns gold
They left muddy footprints on the carpet
And used the spell book to turn our receptionist
    to a toad.
WE DEMAND COMPENSATION FOR THE LITTER
And an apology for making our Griffin cry
Your hyperactive hooligans used foul language
And opened the black hole in room 114.
You and your family are hereby banned from
    our museum
Our doors are shut to your darn devil brood
The police will be in touch about our complaints
    shortly
An additional charge will be made to employ a
    werewolf hunter
Binky was a loved pet and museum favorite
The building is a lesser place since they let him escape
And his many midnight murders are solely
    on your hands.

Minimalism:
A Handbook of Minimalist Genre Poetic Forms

This handbook contains articles about how to write various minimalist poetry forms such as scifaiku, senryu, sijo, haibun, empat perkataan, ghazals, cinquain, cherita, rengays, rengu, octains, tanka, threesomes, and many more. Each article is written by an expert in that particular poetry form.

Teri Santitoro, aka sakyu, who assembled this handbook, has been the editor of Scifaikuest since 2003.

https://www.hiraethsffh.com/product-page/minimalism-a-handbook-of-minimalist-genre-poetic-forms

Movie Review: Raven's Hollow
Lee Clark Zumpe

How can one not admire the works of Edgar Allan Poe? As both a horror writer and lifelong fan of the genre, I can attest to the fact that his influence on the genre is immeasurable. But his literary contributions are not limited to a single pigeonhole. In addition to his well-known tales of the macabre, he basically invented detective fiction and was among the earliest writers to dabble in the field of science fiction.

Poe died in 1849 under somewhat enigmatic circumstances. He was only 40 years old. There is disagreement as to the exact number of tales he completed in his abbreviated lifetime. Most agree that the number falls between 60 and 70. His stories have been collected in countless omnibuses and anthologies over the last 173 years. Many have been adapted into feature films, comic books, and graphic novels. The Alan Parsons Project's debut album, "Tales of Mystery and Imagination," features retellings of Poe's tales such as "The Tell Tale Heart," and "The Cask of Amontillado."

I can't remember when or where I first discovered Poe. It may have been one of Roger Corman's Poe cycle adaptations: "The Masque of the Red Death," released in 1964, would have been broadcast on WTOG's Saturday afternoon TV horror movie series "Creature Feature," hosted by the Tampa Bay legend Dr. Paul Bearer (as portrayed by Dick Bennick Sr.). On the other hand, I may have found Poe in the classroom at my Tyrone area elementary school. In the 1970s, Pendulum Press published a series of comic book adaptations — similar in presentation to Classics Illustrated — under the imprint Now Age Books. Among the books in this series was "The Best of Poe," which included "The Fall of the House of Usher."

It wasn't until college that I understood what made Poe's work so appealing to me: his execution of a "unity of effect." It is a philosophy of composition I strive to follow in my own fiction.

I can see Poe's "unity of effect" at work in the new film "Raven's Hollow." Directed by Christopher Hatton, this movie is not an adaptation of one of Poe's tales. Instead, it is a work of fiction using Poe as its central character.

Set in 1830, the film follows West Point military Cadet Edgar Allan Poe and four other cadets as they travel through upstate New York beneath cold, gray skies. On their journey, they discover a dying man who has been tied to a sacrificial rack made from branches. His killer eviscerated him. Before he dies, he utters a single word: "Raven."

At the urging of Poe, played by actor William Moseley, the cadets retrieve the man's corpse and search for a nearby community. They soon stumble upon Raven's Hollow — and quickly conclude that the man was trying to convey the name of his home.

As soon as they ride into the town, they sense something is amiss. The town seems nearly deserted, and its few inhabitants are clearly reluctant to speak to the visitors. Their statements and demeanor suggest they are hiding sinister secrets.

Again at Poe's insistence, the cadets decide to stay in Raven's Hollow to determine who is responsible for the man's brutal murder. Poe becomes infatuated with Charlotte (Melanie Zanetti), daughter of the town's innkeeper Elizabet (Kate Dickie). Usher (Oberon

K.A. Adjepong) — a resident of the town who is connected to Charlotte and Elizabet — warns the cadets that they are in danger and advises them to leave as soon as possible.

Usher reveals that there is an evil entity tormenting the village. He calls it a raven, but claims it is not an animal. What he describes is a supernatural force, though he cannot decide if it is a spirit or a demon. Most of the cadets do not initially believe Usher's claims. Nevertheless, one of the visitors disappears during the night. Poe leads a hasty search the following morning, discovering the grisly remains of his comrade buried beneath floorboards in an abandoned building outside of the town.

Even after finding the mutilated body, Poe discounts the idea of a supernatural entity as the architect of these crimes. The viewer, however, knows better.

Hatton imbues the film with heavy gothic ambiance. I think he may well have used the opening lines from Poe's "The Fall of the House of Usher" to visualize the milieu: "During the whole of a dull, dark, and soundless day in the autumn of the year, when the clouds hung oppressively low in the heavens, I had been passing alone, on horseback, through a singularly dreary tract of country; and at length found myself, as the shades of the evening drew on, within view of the melancholy House of Usher." Raven's Hollow is an entire village of buildings that — like the house of Roderick Usher — evoke "a sense of insufferable gloom."

Unfortunately, while Hatton put extra effort into making the atmosphere effectively gloomy, he shortchanged most of the characters populating those grim environs. Poe and his colleagues are thinly developed caricatures, and it is difficult to foster much sympathy for them even as they slip deeper into peril.

The townsfolk are mostly presented as untrustworthy and erratic. Even their testimonies are shown to be unreliable throughout the film. It's unclear to know who among them is well-meaning and who is potentially hostile.

The biggest issue though is the fact that Moseley is outright distracting as Poe. He's a square peg and Hatton is trying to mash him into a round hole. He simply doesn't mirror Poe in any sense that the viewing audience might expect. That may have been intentional, but it kept me from connecting with the story's protagonist because it caused such cerebral dissonance.

"Poe is remembered to history as a pallid, haunted figure, but long before that he was a bright and distinguished West Point cadet," the film's production notes states. "The events surrounding his sudden discharge have never been explained. Here is where our story is set. In Raven's Hollow, Poe becomes the central character of an imaginative Gothic horror that delves into the origins of his dark fiction and fractured psyche. It is the fantastic tale of how Poe became Poe."

But Moseley's Poe doesn't feel like Poe — and that's a significant fail in terms of the film's ability to maintain its hold over the viewer. That problem is further exacerbated by a barrage of Easter eggs — such as calling one of the characters Usher. Hatton is either suggesting that story seeds fall at Poe's feet every few minutes or he is just trying to be clever by inserting as many references and allusions as possible to appease well-read viewers. There are so many citations that I started to imagine a Pop-Up Video version, ala VH1, with onscreen footnotes interrupting the plot.

The film does feature some outstanding performances, including Adjepong's portrayal of Usher and Dickie's Elizabet. Also delivering a solid showing is David Hayman. Hayman plays the town's eccentric doctor, known for taking perverse pleasure in dissecting cadavers. The fact that he somehow looks like Ian Holm playing Bilbo Baggins makes his character even more wickedly weird.

Even with its flaws, "Raven's Hollow" is entertaining. While the characters could be better cultivated and the plot could be more cohesive and less confusing, the creepy, brooding tone goes a long way toward making it appealing — if not as an attention-grabbing, thought-provoking tale of the macabre, then at least as a fascinating curio that speculates on Poe's source of inspiration.

"Raven's Hollow" debuted on Shudder Sept. 22, 2022.

INFO BOX
"Raven's Hollow"
Genres: Mystery, horror
Director: Christopher Hatton
Cast: Melanie Zanetti, William Moseley, Kate Dickie, Callum Woodhouse, Mathis Landwehr, Oberon K.A. Adjepong, Kyle Rowe, and David Hayman
Release date: Sept. 22, 2022
Run time: 98 minutes
Not rated

The Cliff
R L Raymond

Her breath hangs
    toxic
in the bottleneck
frozen at the mouth
of the bridge
a siren's whisper
    floating –
        a foggy invitation

Immunity refracts
in the mist
prismatic patterns
on an upturned hand

She flirts with him
her incantation
condensed
malignant

A siren's whisper
echoed in the pines
the river's edge
    frosty
the snow knee-deep –
he shrugs and backs away
    from her
        for another

Featured Poet: Yuliia Vereta

Notes from the far

It is not mentioned in the Directory of planets.
There are no minerals, no water, no vegetation.
Inhabited by low-level robots of obsolete types,
out of production for dozens of earthly years.
Thanks to sunflower oil I made friends with one
With indicators on his forehead and wrists.
He is capricious and touchy, but knows gears.
Civilization is primitive, not computerized.
Agriculture is entirely absent. So are the beasts.
The planet is a flat gray ball, without mountains,
air or oceans, with a surface covered with dust.
This is a decent place for my aging and blackout.
During the flight around the mighty Reynold-V,
I got tiny bacteria crawling into my lubricant.
They turn it into sick abrasive solution. I'm rusting.
Solar engines don't work. I now hold on the wires.
Want to give the locals permission to dismantle me
and use parts for the good. They are kind to me.
They look like the ancestors I have never had.

Once a Fortnight

The houses tremble at the appearance of the tram
whose aim is to not let us die.
That is how we get what we need here, in the most
remote areas of what is left.

Drinking water, gel for the nostrils, 20% disinfectant,
sunscreen and dry rations.
There are always too few of them: sometimes we
manage, sometimes we don't.

Yellow air and fine dust creep into the asphalt cracks
and under the whitewash.
It even gets under the skin, into tired hearts, passing
lungs and clogged filters.

Workers in swamp-green uniforms unload the goods,
boxes land on the sand.
Everything edible is in tubes, powder, compressed
tablets, dense jelly and cans.

They pump drinking water and pour it into the tanks
with a hose, *dou* by *dou*.
If someone told me that my life would look like this, I
would never believe them.

I was like everyone else, an ordinary passer-by
covering my face with the collar.
A clerk with a family and a job that I never
appreciated, before they were gone.

With a deafening roar, the empty tram pulls away,
iron horns resting on wires.
It leaves us with gifts from the more fortunate districts
in the South of Lands.

Two rails run into distance; they hide in dust, where the metropolis used to be.
I follow our savior with my eyes; it disappears and makes me pass out helplessly.

I don't have the strength to stand up, hope to find at least the strength to forget.
Find the strength not to live in the past, in its sweet air of dark nights and shade.

The North

Where I was born the main color was white
The sun was indistinguishable from the moon.
Where I was born, I always went to the north -
Because there no other side has been invented.

We had hymns of dancing madness in us,
Created by those who will not answer our prayers.
It's a cure for an old age, medicine for the tired,
Always invigorates better than any whip.

These madmen taught us how to live together,
We have been blessed to breed in the darkness.
We all want to go up, we all want to get higher,
But the engineers of my body decided I can only walk.

Over the years here I have become wiser.
I am treated with wine and forest silence.
Jasper stalk replaced my compass and a lifeline,
But I'm still looking for a vaccine for pain.

For any money, no matter how much it costs,
I will buy it from you, if you bring it. Please do.
So that I can see southern dreams in the north,
then melt like the snow and seep into the soil like life.

Textures of the Future

Down the Milky Way's L16,
On the fifth nautical kilometer,
Right next to "Sputnik and Sons",
Floats the tavern you can find me in, -
"The home of the Weird" is pretty precise
As for name of the ship full of humans like me.

After the Age Out-of-Touch,
When I got born for the first time,
It became hard to find someone with
Collagen bones, fiber muscles and tongue,
Not carrying around the oxygen kit they now call
"The first aid for the naturally born human younglings".

I am proud to still possess
Fifty vertebrae, fours thumbs,
And a lung strong enough to turn
Smoke into what makes my organism
Work as one of the best Carnall-70's watches
With no need to daily refill or filter my hemoplasma.

However, the rules here
Are pretty strict and level-2
Species as well as the mutants
Including the cyborgs, are not allowed,
So if you are lucky enough to be one of those
I am sorry you can't enter the place I am talking about.

Same thing for the oods,
The judoons, the mechanoids,
Alpha Centaurans, ogrons, and quarks;
For those human beings that were transformed

Or updated in any way the place is open and ready
To serve the best soy drinks and bean cutlets in
space.

So, just in case, if you are
Looking for me on a regular
Workday, discharged and hungry,
Take a ride to "The home of the Weird"
Where polyurethane chew gums taste three
Times longer that any creature could ever imagine.

Teleporter Talk
Lauren McBride

All of us teleport pads
are left with a wisp
of consciousness
from everyone we
have transported.
Mine are friendly.
Behind me, there's
an ongoing fight.
Started a few years
back. The rest of us
can't hear ourselves
think! If only someone
inherently logical
or peaceful would
step on that pad,
the noisy arguing
might finally stop!

Adrift
Albert N. Katz
(for Kel-El, Moses, Frankenstein's creature, Alan Kurdi, all the others sent adrift)

launched
    with chants and fears
he saw black
    for the longest time
swaddled
    in his cocoon, entombed
fading
    in and out of consciousness
remembering
    faces, the touch of hugs
the stench
    of burning flesh in his nose, on his clothes
voices
    begging him not to forget the golden towers
    (or maybe just the fables of golden towers)
questioning
    are there others adrift? are they waiting, like me,
    for some beach, a jolt, a landing
wondering
    will I be rescued and nurtured?
or
    treated as a monster?
alone
    in a distant foreign land?

Greek Amazon Woman
By Sandy DeLuca

Amazon Warrior
Deborah Sheldon

Philantha sees the horses first,
beneath a tree, penned by branches.
No one about. She advances,
warily, ignoring her thirst,
her hunger, the wound she has nursed
since the doomed battle to save Troy;
her arm cut by a Greek, a boy.
She repaid his sword with her spear
and ran him through, twice, stole his gear
and fled. She is without convoy.

A hot cloudless sky bakes the plain.
Her feet crunch dead meadow flowers.
Nervous horses snort. One cowers
from her hand. She sings, pats his mane,
he calms. Oh, their Trojan campaign
was for naught; she'll ride home at speed
to Thermiskyra on this steed.
From the grasses, a man sits up.
Shackled, naked, dirty; a pup
that poses no threat. "Hah! Take heed!"

He says, "Go, and flee while you can
before my mistresses come back.
You're an Amazon! They'll attack
and kill you outright. Your daft plan
of horse-stealing is dafter than
your allegiance to King Priam.
Woman, how could you be so dumb?"

Philantha surveys the man's chain,
says "I'll free you, then leave this plain."
He points, laughs. "Too late! You'll succumb."

She looks to the dirt road nearby—
no one. She listens, hears nothing.
She'll open the corral and spring
upon this horse, which does not shy
from her touch. Then she looks up high
into the tree. Its leaves are fouled
with shit, as if birds have crowd'd
the branches. The tree holds no birds.
The man laughs, "Can't you see their turds?"
Shapes are silhouetted by cloud.

Shapes of bulky birds, advancing,
big as vultures, but these are worse.
Harpies. Philantha breathes a curse
as the hag-birds approach, winging
to land, Philantha's wound stinging,
and her only weapon a spear.
"You shouldn't have been cavalier,"
mocks the man. Both harpies touch down,
awkwardly, like bats, totter, frown
at Philantha with a cold sneer.

Breasts, arms, typical of woman,
each face as white as a flayed skull,
puckered eyes blinking dank and dull,
lipless mouths flexing, inhuman.
The man snickers, "Look what you've done,
Amazon, secured your demise.
Anyone trying to fight – dies."
Philantha lifts her spear, presses
her toes in the dirt, muscles flex

for the onslaught. She moves crabwise.

"Girl, I'm Odarg," says the big one,
"You need to make peace with your gods."
Philantha says, "You lack the odds,
you are two, but you'll both be gone."
"Kill her now!" shouts the man, "have fun
with her corpse, then chomp on her guts."
The small harpy says, "No smugness!
Call a truce. She might be wounded,
but take care! I have concluded
that she'll slay us all with quick cuts."

Odarg snarls, "Drop spear, Amazon."
She replies, "Come take it from me,"
but she's backing close to the tree.
The Amazon looks weak and wan—
This battle is already won.
Hah! Odarg smiles at her sister.
"We'll give the dregs to your mister,"
she remarks while she shows her nails,
each claw poisoned as the folktales
describe. "No one to assist her."

Convinced, the little one snarls, leaps.
Quick, strong, Philantha lifts the spear,
which cleaves through to the stringy rear
of the small harpy. Dark blood seeps
into the dry soil. Odarg weeps.
"Take the horse," Odarg cries, "and flee,
but somewhere on the road there'll be
a host of us waiting for you.
We'll smash and bash you, black and blue.
Rue the day you walked to my tree."

Weak, ill, Philantha mounts the horse
and trots from the meadow, leaving
there a harpy and man wailing,
their grief fresh. Philantha, of course,
knows the harpies will chase in force.
Will infection kill her instead?
Faint, she lets the horse have its head.
Trotting north-east, towards her home,
the hooves clip-clop like metronome.
Philantha frets in darkest dread.

The harpies will advance like owls.
Soft and quiet, with sharp talons drawn,
they'll assail by night or by dawn.
Philantha knows this in her bowels.
Her horse is tired, and evil prowls
about her as the sunset gloams.
She steels herself by seeing homes
in her mind's eye: there, the Black Sea
with boats working nets by the quay
and, by the shore, the catacombs.

Stranded Alien
Jan Cronos

ennui and fear in arid earthly winter
alone and isolate
expatriate from sun swept watery world
an influx of despair
of cold of susurrations in icy air
that lead to desperation as she
shivers by the frosty river's edge

a floe
a sheet of floating ice
a flow of chilling fog wolf gray
obscures the light
faint rays from sinking Sol
dazzles her sea damp eyes and mind
misgives, gives in to sadness
overwhelming as

she plunges in
her swirling head beneath the wintry waves
at last she's numb to feelings then
euphoria as images of home world rise, falling
as consciousness departs

Columbus
Gary Every

We were all taught lies in school.
Columbus never believed the world was flat.
Most people of the time didn't believe it either.
Aristarchus had already proven that the earth
    was round.
Eratosthenes had correctly calculated the earth's
    circumference.
Columbus proposed that Eratosthenes was wrong,
that all of civilization had been mistaken for centuries,
that the earth was really 10,000 miles smaller;
a number which conveniently removes the
    Pacific Ocean.
When Columbus landed in the Caribbean,
It was exactly where his calculations told him
China was supposed to be.
No wonder he was confused.
People also forget that Columbus
made four journeys to the New World
and that during the second journey
he was arrested and placed in chains.
Once the ship left Cuba
The captain requested they remove the chains,
because where would Columbus escape to
while the ship was at sea.
Columbus refused, demanding to sail all the way
    to Spain
bound in shackles and chains.

Galileo Galilei grew bored of staring through
    telescopes
and wrote a playful student's thesis
precisely calculating with precision

the dimensions of Hell as laid out in Dante's Inferno,
even composing complex equations to discern
the exact angle of Satan's bunghole
so that Virgil and Dante might exit Hell safely.
Most of medieval Europe believed
that when Lucifer was expelled from heaven,
he and his fallen angels plummeted to earth
as a burning meteorite, crashing into the Earth
    so hard
that they burrowed all the way to the center
    of the earth,
reaching the molten fires at the core,
residing along the shores of the Lake of Fire.
All that displaced earth had created a giant mountain
which towered above the South Pole.
At the peak of this mountain God placed
    the Garden of Eden.
Four mighty rivers were said to flow from the Garden.
On his fourth journey, when Columbus reached
    South America
he stumbled upon the Orinoco River
whose confluence pushed his ships unbelievably fast.
Columbus was convinced
he had stumbled upon one of the rivers flowing
    out of Eden.
All one had to do was journey upriver to rediscover
    Paradise.
never mind that there were allegedly cherubim
    with flaming swords
guarding the gates.
No one took Columbus seriously.
Columbus died broke, ashamed and slightly crazy,
demanding that he be buried in his shackles
    and chains
angry that his navigational achievements
had not received their proper acclaim.
Galileo's precise calculations aside

I can think of no better metaphor for hell
than going to the grave clad in shackles and chains,
refusing to abandon outdated beliefs.
Perhaps that is why we do not wander
    among the stars,
the same stars Columbus used to navigate by.
Perhaps it is time to remove our shackles and chains.

Three Legged Cat
Gary Every

Ever since he lost his back leg he walks without grace
in a hippity hoppity sort of gait
prowling the yard for lizards and birds
meowing for snacks and attention.
An attack by a rogue neighborhood dog
cost him one leg and one of his nine lives.
He has eight lives remaining and eight legs too,
five invisible legs reaching into other dimensions,
claws raking demons or receiving pedicures
    from angels.
One pair of ethereal limbs continuously kneads God
as one leg twitches like a tail in the afterworld,
keeping him spiritually balanced
in this life and the next.

Those from Ryugu
Andrew Najberg

My daughter and I watch the Ryugu probe land
with chute and smoke. Humans learned from religion
to work through avatars: gods never stick fingers in
soil.

I want to tell my daughter that one day
We will travel to the stars, but she yawns,
asks if we could fly to the sun. I confess:

stars aren't things we land on. I don't really know
what is. I hope to see the first person walk on Mars,
but perhaps the future will strip our rind and pulp.

Leave us as seeds without soil. Mother Nature doesn't
make the promises we make our children. We must
find the water we will drink. Natural states leave

parched throats and cracked lips, and my daughter
smacks her lips, flutters her lids, rolls into sleep.
Her dreams strong enough to fuel a rocket,

I lay her in the glow of her constellation nightlight,
imagine she sees herself among the stars as our best
headlines proclaim only that *I hope so,*

as records highs break like summer clay
when the shadows pass.

My Electric Lycanthropy
RK Rugg

My electric lycanthropy
lusts for the Moon,
but don't you for one moment imagine
that faraway orb, pale and stark, is in control.
Luna and her sisters
    (Ocean. Nature.)
know of me, but don't know me.

No, I am wolf by blood.
My transformation is kindled from within,
    not imposed from without.
Ironic, yes, since what is blood
but the analog (a contemporary translation)
    of that ancient ocean
from whence we evolved?
What is blood
but our most foundational tie to nature, the very
    reason for the beating
of our hearts?
What is blood
but a manifestation of the cycle that is the
    feminine birthright?

Nevertheless.
The wolf blood is different than, separate from.
This is the blood that tears and rips and rends.
Forget what you think you know
from fairytales, myths and legends.
My hands and head are all that change.
The rest stays human, naked and unashamed.
Don't ask me why, that's just how it is.

I keep me in a tower built from rough-hewn granite,
    covered in ivy.
So there's your fairytale setting, if you insist on that
sort of thing.
When I take the chains off,
I'm free to run wild but only within the stony confines;
the tower has no door, nor true window.
There is only a narrow slit in the wall,
high and out of reach,
> ('So high, too high,' the blood growls,
>   but doesn't really mean it--it's more performative
>   than sincere)

through which I spy upon her
ever-changing never-changing face.

Moonlight drips down the walls.
I bathe in the puddles. And howl.

The wolf has been. The wolf is now and for
    some years to come.
Someday the tower will crumble
and the chains will flake away to rust.
But I'll be gone by then and
the last trace of the blood will be
a faint black stain on the floor.
'The grave settles all debts,' they say
and that's where my responsibility ends.
That's the happy-ever-after for me and
my electric lycanthropy.

The Old House
R L Raymond

She has memorized the walls
    of this tiny room
        crouched in dust
the patina of fear and isolation
nearly scrubbed from the moldings
with grains of sand and a sliver of broken glass

She hurries to record the details -
why the paint is chipped
    from the frame
why the mouseprints
    in the dirt
        only travel one way

If the ogre opens the door
she will hide the broken hourglass
    palmed from a high shelf
she will obscure the work
    with her body -
the past stories not quite retold

***

She hopes that dinner will be late
that the stale bread
    tepid water
        and chocolate long chalky
will wait a little longer
so she can write their final chapter

Then when the ogre opens the door
    and she is done
    and she has strength
she will throw the last handful of sand
    and chips of glass into its dying eyes
        and run

She has memorized the walls
she has retold the stories
    of those who came before
her footprints in the dunes will travel one way
    her own weakened voice will swell
        with the triumph of a collective escape

Disintegration
Christopher Hivner

Wake up.
We have to go.
The danger is real,
illusions will lead us
down the wrong corridor.
Wake up.
I can hear the water,
we won't escape this time
like the last.
Can't you hear that?
A siren about us,
I told you we need to go.
They've been following us,
a day behind
until tonight.
Wake up.
I know how they got in,
not what you think,
They're too clever
by half,
but we can still survive
if you'll wake up.

Never mind,
too late.
I'm going to join you
in the sleep chamber,
take a hit
of the gas and
drop.
They'll follow us

into the warp,
but I have a plan.
Hold your body together
when the disintegration begins,
swim in the brine
with me
until we reach the cave,
we can hide there
no matter how many dives
they make.
We can hide.
It won't feel like living,
but we won't
be dead.

You; in the City of Desire
Goran Lowie

Near the end of your journey you finally discover
directions to the ancient meteor-city of Markusis,
you close your eyes and recite a prayer before
going into cryosleep, entertaining zero-gravity dreams.

When you finally arrive, you find
golden birds that taste of homesick love,
women bathing in radiating water,
stone trees emitting shades of lust,
unrequited love in bleary taverns.

After days of pleasure
one day you wake up and find the city's true ethos;
its heart awakens desires from deep within you
surrounding you with unrealized, new yearnings
while at first you believe no desire was lost
you quickly come to realize that your longing
is never met; you work as a cutter of amethysts
you believe your labor satisfies your desire,
a delusional
belief that you are enjoying Markusis,
while you are really
only its subservient slave.

Scrying
Andrew Najberg

My wife tells me in the lamplight
after everyone else has gone to sleep
that sometimes she hopes

our children won't have children
because they will suffer what
we leave behind, that we are

the last lucky ones to whom plenty
means more than we need
rather than more than we have.

I can't comprehend how my hypothetical
grandchildren might live. They'll use
food science as one word. Land

on asteroids, Mars, control computers
with their minds. Maybe they'll
pre-program their dreams like mixed tapes.

My daughter and I talk about this
and that; her classes, my day, the movie
we watch, but could we evolve beyond

mouths and simply think with each other?
Can we still have hands that can hold?
My wife and I lie on the couch, tired,

the sound low. Outside, trees on the slopes,
millions of cicadas and crickets in them,
the darkness shattered infinitely in their song.

The Bones of the Machine
Christopher Hivner

I fell into
the connected thoughts
of the collective
hive mind

Switches and wires
the continuum
loads information
broken jagged

Where are my own thoughts
among the circuitry
neon lights
point me in the wrong direction

circled
whispers
intruder
eliminate

The bones of the machine
crack from pressure
Klaxons shriek
original thought breaks through

Am I free?
the dials turn
the switches click
the hive can't find me

Connected thoughts
harvested to serve the collective
free thought
marked for destruction

I am out
escaped through an unused port
echoes of the chatter follow me
until I hear only myself

I fell into the abyss
saw monsters with fiber optic teeth
they couldn't catch me
because I knew their every thought

www.ingramcontent.com/pod-product-compliance
Lightning Source LLC
LaVergne TN
LVHW012037060526
838201LV00061B/4658